The Tide
Comes In

KINGFISHER

NEW YORK

KINGFISHER
LONDON & NEW YORK

Copyright © Kingfisher 2012
Published in the United States by Kingfisher,
175 Fifth Ave., New York, NY 10010
Kingfisher is an imprint of Macmillan Children's Books, London.
All rights reserved.

Written and designed by Dynamo Ltd.

Distributed in the U.S. and Canada by Macmillan, 1
75 Fifth Ave., New York, NY 10010

Library of Congress Cataloging-in-Publication data has been applied for.

ISBN 978-0-7534-7003-9

Kingfisher books are available for special promotions and premiums. For details contact:
Special Markets Department, Macmillan, 175 Fifth Ave., New York, NY 10010.

For more information, please visit www.kingfisherbooks.com

Printed in China
9 8 7 6 5 4 3 2 1
1TR/0612/HH/-/140MA

Contents

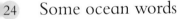

How big is the ocean?

Almost three fourths of Earth, our planet, is covered by ocean.

The ocean is made up of five different parts—the Pacific, the Atlantic, the Indian, the Southern, and the Arctic. These smaller oceans flow together to make one very big world ocean.

Ocean facts

- The largest ocean is the Pacific.
- The coldest ocean is the Arctic.
- The deepest ocean is the Pacific.

The words *sea* and *ocean* can
be used to mean the same thing.
But scientists use the word *sea*
to describe part of an ocean.

Why is the ocean salty?

The water in the ocean tastes salty because it has salt in it.

Rainwater and rivers pick up tiny amounts of salt from rocks and soil as they run down to the ocean. They bring this salt to the ocean, which becomes salty.

Salty facts

- The saltiest ocean water is in the Red Sea.
- The least salty water in the ocean is found in the polar regions.
- If all of the salt in the ocean was spread out over Earth's land surface, it would be as high as seven houses.

These people are collecting salt from the ocean. We use salt collected in this way on our food.

7

Where do waves come from?

The wind blows across the surface of the ocean and makes ripples. These ripples are called waves.

The stormier the weather—and the more wind there is— the bigger the waves become.

Wave facts

- The biggest wave ever recorded was in Alaska in 1958. It was more than 1,700 ft. (500m) high.

- In places such as Hawaii, surfers can ride waves as tall as 50 feet (15 meters).

Waves can travel
thousands of miles
across the ocean before
reaching the shore

Why is there sand on the beach?

Sand is actually tiny pieces of rock and shell that have been broken up by the ocean and the rain.

The waves wash these broken pieces onto the shore, making sandy beaches.

Sand facts

- Not every beach has yellow sand. Some beaches have pink or even black sand.
- Black sand is made up of tiny pieces of black rock, which comes from volcanoes.
- Pink sand has many tiny pieces of pink coral in it.

Sandcastles are easier
to build when the
sand is slightly wet

11

Why does the tide come in and go out?

The Moon causes the tide to come in and go out.

Like a magnet, the Moon tries to pull things that are on Earth toward it. This makes the ocean move closer to or farther from the shore.

Tide facts

- When the tide goes out, we can see more of the beach.
- The tide going out uncovers rock pools, where many plants and animals live.
- Limpets cling to rocks, so the tide can't pull them off when it goes out.

The tide comes in
and goes out every
day. It never stops.

What does the ocean floor look like?

The bottom of the ocean looks like land, but underwater.

There are mountains, valleys, and flat plains, just as there are on the rest of Earth.

Ocean bed facts

- The deepest part of the ocean is the Mariana Trench in the Pacific Ocean.
- Almost all of the ocean floor has a temperature of 39°F (4°C)—that is as cold as a refrigerator!
- All of the underwater mountains are connected, making them the longest mountain range in the world.

Mauna Kea, in Hawaii,
is the world's largest
underwater mountain.
Its top part rises above
the water.

What is a coral reef?

Coral is made by tiny animals called polyps that live in colonies. When they die, they leave their skeletons behind. These hard skeletons build up to form pieces of coral.

Over many hundreds of years, the pieces of coral grow into huge reefs.

Great Barrier Reef facts

- The Great Barrier Reef in the Pacific Ocean, just off the coast of Australia, is the biggest coral reef in the world.
- More than 1,500 different kinds of fish live there.
- The reef is made from more than 400 different types of corals.

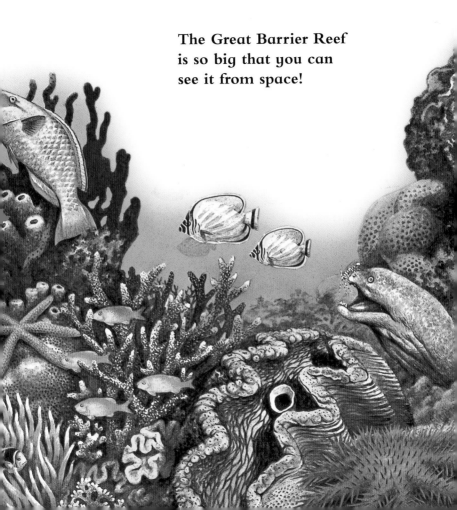

The Great Barrier Reef
is so big that you can
see it from space!

Does anything live at the bottom of the ocean?

The bottom of the ocean is a cold, dark place, but it is home to many amazing animals, including the giant squid.

The creatures that live down there have special features to help them survive.

Secrets of the deep

- Most creatures that live at the bottom of the ocean have soft bodies. This helps them live in very deep water.
- Many of the fish are brightly colored or glow. This helps them attract food in the dark.
- Small creatures called snail fish have been found living in a crack more than 4 miles (7km) below the ocean floor.

People don't live at the bottom of the ocean, but there are man-made objects down there. All sorts of things have been found in shipwrecks—including treasure!

How can we explore under the ocean?

Submarines are used to explore under the ocean, but they can't travel very far down.

If we want to look deeper, we have to use smaller craft called submersibles.

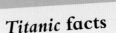

Titanic facts

- When the *Titanic* sailed, it was the biggest ship ever built.
- The *Titanic* hit an iceberg on its very first trip.
- The *Titanic* sank in the Atlantic Ocean, and its wreck is still there today.

The *Titanic* was a huge ship that sank in 1912. Its wreck was found almost 2.5 miles (4km) under the ocean by a submersible called *Alvin*.

What do you know about the ocean?

You can find all of the answers to these questions in this book.

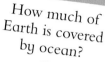

How much of Earth is covered by ocean?

Are waves bigger or smaller when it is stormy?

Are there mountains under the ocean?

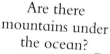

Why do some creatures at the bottom of the ocean glow?

Where is the biggest coral reef in the world?

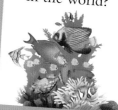

What color is sand?

Can a submarine go to the very bottom of the ocean?

Some ocean words

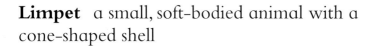

Coast   The area of land near the ocean.

Limpet   a small, soft-bodied animal with a cone-shaped shell

Shipwreck   The remains of a ship after it has sunk.

Shore   The land at the very edge of the ocean.

Submersible   A type of small, underwater craft that can explore deep under the ocean.

Surfer   Someone who uses a special board, called a surfboard, to ride the ocean waves.

Tide   The movement of the ocean closer to and farther from the shore.

24